Ko te whiwhi reo i roto i tenei ao hou – To have a voice in the modern world

EPIDEMICS THROUGH TIME

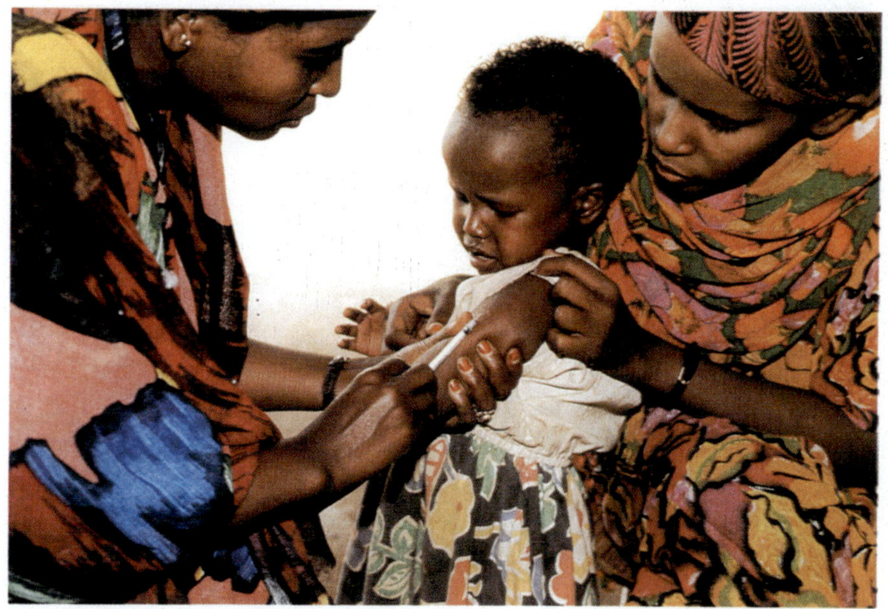

RUTH NAUMANN

Australia • Brazil • Japan • Korea • Mexico • Singapore • Spain • United Kingdom • United States

CONTENTS

RAP ON WITH HISTORY

The Black Death was a disease. It came to Europe in 1347 and killed millions of people. European history from about 500 to about 1500 is called the **Middle Ages**. This time was after the Ancient History of the Greeks and Romans and before Modern History. If you had been alive in 1347, you would have been living in **medieval** times.

Hey hey hey, let's rap on with history
It's real cool and it ain't no mystery
Now this Black Death was pretty bad stuff
It made for life bein' way too tough
Inside their houses people were dead
And on the door were crosses in red
No better killer had ever been
Must have been a grave-digger's dream
Must have been an awesome scene ....

Where the Black Death fits in to History

- **31–33 A.D.** Christ's teaching and crucifixion
- **43** Romans start conquest of Britain
- **570** Birth of Mohammed
- **1209** St Francis of Assissi founds Order of Friars
- **1212** Children's Crusade
- **1215** King John grants Magna Carta
- **1271** Marco Polo goes to China
- **1337** Start of 100 Years' War between England and France
- **1347** Black Death hits Europe
- **1350** Fleet of canoes in Maori tradition
- **1431** Joan of Arc burnt at stake
- **1492** Columbus reaches New World
- **1588** Spanish Armada defeated
- **1605** Guy Fawkes & Gunpowder Plot
- **1655** Great Plague of London
- **1769** Cook visits New Zealand
- **1815** Battle of Waterloo
- **1840** Treaty of Waitangi
- **1861–65** American Civil War
- **1869** Suez Canal opened
- **1918** Influenza epidemic
- **1914–18** World War I
- **1925** Bad Polio epidemic in New Zealand
- **1939–45** World War II
- **1945** Atomic bombs on Japan
- **1953** Edmund Hillary climbs Mt Everest
- **1969** First person on the moon
- **1984** First AIDS cases notified in New Zealand
- **1994** Plague in India
  1995 Ebola virus in Zaire
- **1995** New Zealand wins America's Cup

SKILL / PŪKENGA

Working With a Time-line

1 Brainstorm the time-line to find out what happened at each event.

2 Choose ten events, including the Black Death, from the time-line to make your own mini time-line.

3 Mark in your date of birth and another two events that are important to you.

4 Colour code it this way –

red – exploration and travel
blue – loss of life
green – religion
yellow – fighting
orange – political
brown – personal

5 Choose one of the events and compose a rap song about it.

TECHNOLOGY COMES TO THE MIDDLE AGES

Medieval people would be amazed at the technology that is available today. They had few resources to cope with the Black Death. Most people saw no changes that made their lives easier. Yet these five inventions were important in the Middle Ages. They helped spread the Black Death too because they gave people more mobility and increased contact between people. Ships from Europe could now sail to Asia to trade. The Black Death came to Europe from Asia on board trading ships.

IMPORTANT MEDIEVAL INVENTIONS

Rigid Horse Collar
The new collar meant the horse could pull heavier loads without being strangled.

Stirrups
Now soldiers were able to fight much better on horseback. In the Middle Ages, mounted soldiers were called knights.

Lateen Sail
The old square sail was good only when the wind blew behind the ship. But this new triangular sail went well in all winds.

Magnetic Compass
Now a navigator could navigate a ship even when he could not see land or other guides such as the sun and stars.

Sternpost Rudder
Oars near the stern used to steer ships. But the new rudder could steer much bigger ships and sail them safely in rough seas.

SKILL / PŪKENGA

Group Enquiry

1 The box below contains a dozen inventions of the first fifty years of the 20th century –

> penicillin, electric washing machine, DDT, aeroplane, fridge, biro, television, vitamins, plutonium, computer, transistor radio, Model T Ford motor car

Your group is alive in 1347. It is allowed to reach out and take one of these inventions back into the 14th century. Which invention does your group choose and why?

2 Jean Froissart was a Frenchman who was born a few years before the Black Death in Europe. He wrote a history of his own time which he called the 'Chronicle.' When he recorded the Black Death, he wrote that 'a third of the world died.'

If you were keeping a journal about an epidemic that had hit New Zealand and had to write that it had killed a third of the population, what sentence would you write after it?

3 The picture at the bottom of the page shows the Ponte Vecchio in Italy. It is an excellent example of medieval technology. The bridge crosses the river Arno in Florence, which was one of the biggest cities in Europe in the Middle Ages. The bridge was finished just before the Black Death came to Florence.

The Black Death was a contagious disease. The bridge offers a clue why the Black Death killed thousands of people in places like Florence.

AN ENQUIRY INTO SOCIAL ORGANISATION

SKILL / PŪKENGA

Critical Thinking

1 With your group, use the drawings to make a list of ideas about what life in the Middle Ages could have been like.

2 Look at the next chapter to see how accurate your ideas were.

HOW SOCIETY WAS ORGANISED

This is you in 1347 Europe:

You live in a village outside a town. As a peasant, you belong to the group in society that works on the land. Ninety percent of the population are peasants. Another group are the nobles. Their job is to defend people. A third group is the clergy. Their job is to pray and care for Christians.

You have never travelled far, not even to the next village which is 8 km away. Your social life revolves around your own village and market days in town. You speak in a language and accent that only people from your own area can understand.

The world consists of Europe and fringes of Asia. You have never heard of such a place as New Zealand. Or America. For a long time the Church has taught that the Earth is flat. Although some educated people are starting to say that the Earth is round, you still think that if you sailed far enough, you would come to the edge of the world and fall into a bottomless pit.

There is no education for you. A school was started in town once but the teacher was ignorant and used a birch all day to keep order. So you can not read or write. The only books available anyway are those the monks in the nearby abbey have copied by hand. Some of these books are illuminated with brightly coloured drawings. Drawings and wood-cuts have little perspective. This means, for example, that the people in them might be bigger than the buildings and ships they are standing beside.

The houses in town are crammed together in narrow streets. Many families keep animals. The town has walls around it. At night the gates are locked and guarded. Wealthy town houses have servants, and apprentices who sleep in them. People collect their water from wells or the river. Messengers carry letters and town criers shout out the latest news. At least once a week the town has a market. Your family can rent a stall and sell any spare produce.

The lord owns the land on which your family works. There are almost a hundred servants living in the lord's castle. The family dresses in silks and has banquets. Even the females ride horses and hunt with falcons. One of the daughters had a marriage arranged for her when she was a child. She had been widowed two times by the time she was thirteen.

You live in a hovel. It is a single storey wooden house with two rooms. It has a thatch roof. Straw covers the floor. You eat porridge for breakfast, bread with maybe a bit of cheese for lunch and pottage for dinner. Your mother cooks over an open fire. She makes your bread at home and bakes it in the oven owned by the lord. You wear simple homespun clothes of linen and wool and a hood like a cowl.

There are no fences or hedges on the land. The open fields are divided into strips. Each family is allowed a certain number of strips in the different fields. This way every family gets strips of land in the good and bad areas and shares the jobs.

You call yourself a Christian. You think that non-Christians are infidels and Jews especially should be persecuted. The Pope is your spiritual leader. He lives in Avignon in France. Your village has its own church. The priest can make you go to church. If you refuse, the priest can get a special church court to punish you. The priest collects a tithe from your family. This is a tenth of everything that you produce from the land in one year.

The nearby cathedral and abbey have collections of relics. They are clothes and bones thought to have belonged to saints. Many people say these relics can work miracles. You plan one day to visit these shrines and believe that God will reward you for doing this.

You will be lucky to live past your thirties. Many children die at birth. You hardly ever have a bath. You sleep in the same room as the rest of the family. There is a communal family bed

for most members of your family. You have no idea why you get sick. You are frightened of lepers even though they are not allowed to go into inns or bake-houses and are not allowed to wash in streams or walk on narrow footpaths. Every time you hear a bell or a clacker warning you that a leper is approaching, you run away and hide. Last year the city of London passed a law that said lepers are not allowed to go into London. You think this is a good idea.

Conditions all around you are unsanitary. Filth and rubbish are often left in the streets of the town. There are open street sewers. The public latrines have a bad smell. The castle and wealthy town houses have privies that jut out from an outside wall. There is a hole in the bottom which lets waste fall into the river or the ditch. Some town houses have cesspools in the backyard. The cesspools always smell bad and some of them seep into the wells and the river where you get your drinking water. Household urinals drain into street sewers. A law says privies cannot do this but it is often ignored. The abbey's latrine is in a separate building.

Last time you went to town, a baker who had sold underweight bread was in the stocks and a fishmonger who had been selling bad fish was in the pillory. You threw mud and rotten apples at them. A man who had been found drunk was having to walk through the streets wearing a barrel. But the best sight is when a nagging woman or 'scold' is put in the ducking stool and ducked in the village pond. There is an outlaw living in the forest nearby. If he goes into a church he will find sanctuary and his enemies will not be able to touch him. But eventually his hunger and thirst will drive him out.

SKILL / PŪKENGA

Using Information and Drawings

1 Make up a caption for each drawing on pages 6,7,8 and 9.

2 Read the story on pages 8 and 9. Make a full page sketch of the area you live in, in 1347 Europe. Include your house and strips of land. Give your sketch a title.

3 Supply a key for your sketch. Mark in all the points of possible pollution and all the places you might expect to find rats and fleas. These can carry diseases although in 1347 you do not know this.

4 Read the following and then make a drawing to show what a cleric might have looked like at the time of the Black Death.

> In 1342, just before the Black Death, the Archbishop of Canterbury complained about some rich clergy. He said they –
>
> *scorn to wear the tonsure ... and distinguish themselves by effeminate, shoulder-length hair. They walk about in military, rather than clerical dress, with an outer habit, very short and tight-fitting, with long sleeves which do not touch the elbow. Their hair is curled and perfumed, their hoods have lappets of wonderful length. They wear long beards, rings on their fingers and girded belts studded with jewels. Their purses are enamelled gilt, their boots of red and green, peaked and cut in many ways, and their cloaks so furred that there is no distinction between them and laymen.*

5 Make your own copy of this chart and complete it.

Opinion/Fact	A Piece of Supporting Evidence From the Text
Once an infectious disease got inside a town or village, it spread quickly.	
If disease killed large numbers of peasants, society would be disorganised.	
The church was a powerful force in the lives of medieval people.	

EUROPEANS DIDN'T KNOW OF NEW ZEALAND

Nobody knows how many people lived in Europe at the time of the Black Death. A rough estimate is that the population was about 75 million by 1300. But a lot of people died in bad famines between then and the Black Death.
The political map was different to the Europe of today. Germany and Northern Italy, for example, were divided into hundreds of little states rather than big countries. Many states were just cities. And the biggest cities in Europe – Paris, Florence, Venice and Genoa, had populations of only about 100,000 people.

SKILL / PŪKENGA

Mapping

1 Make your own copy of the map of Europe.

2 These ten places were also important at the time of the Black Death. Find out where they are situated and add them to your map.

Bordeaux, Bristol, Crimea, Durham, Lyon, Marseilles, Messina, Montpellier, Seville, Siena

3 In October 1347 trading ships belonging to Genoa sailed homewards. They had been at a port in the Crimea where they had a trading post. If the ships sailed directly to Messina, would they have passed Constantinople OR Rome?

4 Why would places such as Genoa, Palermo, Tunis and Marseilles be spreading points for infectious diseases such as the Black Death?

5 The Black Death spread north up a river to Avignon where the Pope lived. On which river would it have travelled?

6 In the summer of 1348 the Black Death went from Normandy into southern England. What did it have to cross to get there?

7 In the summer of 1348 the Black Death also went north from Italy into Switzerland. What did it have to cross to get there?

8 From Italy the Black Death went into Hungary. In which direction did it travel to get there?

9 In 1349 the Black Death spread to Scotland. At this time Scotland was a separate country. What would have been the last big English city the disease struck before entering Scotland?

10 When the Black Death went to Scandinavia from England, which country out of Norway, Sweden and Finland, is it most likely to have hit first?

How the disease went from Asia to Europe

SKILL / PŪKENGA

Creating a Cartoon Strip

Use the notes in the box to help you make a cartoon strip of at least six frames to show the progress of the Black Death through Europe. Give it a stunning title.

Making Decisions

All your group knows about the 'Black Death' disease is that it is a plague sweeping through Europe and killing people. Talk about the best solutions to these problems.

1 Your group are town councillors. It is April 1348. A ghost ship with a cargo of wool and all the crew dead has drifted into your harbour. So far your town has escaped the Black Death. What should be done about the ship?

2 Your group are physicians and advisers to the Pope. It is March 1348. The plague has just arrived in Avignon. Should the Pope be moved or not?

In October 1347 trading ships from Genoa enter the harbour of Messina in Sicily. At the oars are dead and dying men. They have come from a Black Sea port in the Crimea. The Genoese have a trading post there. The ships tie up at the wharves. Those men who can still walk go ashore. They take the disease with them.

The disease reaches Marseilles in November 1347. By January 1348 it has gone to North Africa through Tunis, westward from Marseilles to Spain and to Genoa and Venice.

In March it goes northward up the Rhône river to Avignon. Between February and May it gets to Narbonne, Montpellier, Carcassonne, Toulouse, Rome and Florence.

Between June and August it gets to Bordeaux, Lyon and Paris. It gets to Seville in July. It spreads to Burgundy and Normandy. Then it goes into southern England. It gets to Bristol in July. It goes from Italy into Switzerland and into Hungary.

In 1349 it goes from Paris to Picardy, Flanders and the Low Countries. It reaches Vienna in March. It gets to London in January and Durham in June. It goes from England to Scotland and Ireland and Norway. From there it goes to Sweden, Denmark, Prussia, Iceland and Greenland and then to northern Russia. It attacks Russia again in 1351.

Once the Black Death gets to a place, it kills people for about six months and then fades away. But in the big cities it dies down in winter and then comes back in spring for another six months. It has gone from most of Europe by the middle of 1350.

Plague comes back many times over the next 350 years although it is never as fierce again. It is not until the early 18th century that it seems to have gone for good but of course it hasn't really.

THE RAT AND FLEA COMBINATION

To start with, the Black Death had no name. People called it the 'Pestilence' or the 'Great Mortality.' It has three forms –

BUBONIC PLAGUE. (Most common type.) Large lymph nodes or buboes (black swellings about the size of an egg or an apple) erupt in the armpits and groin oozing blood and pus. Boils cover the body and black blotches appear on the skin from all the internal bleeding. There is sudden fever, restlessness, confusion and severe pain. Death within five days.

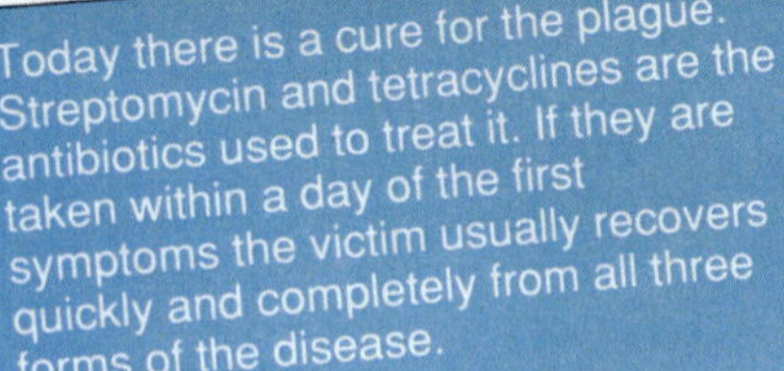

Today there is a cure for the plague. Streptomycin and tetracyclines are the antibiotics used to treat it. If they are taken within a day of the first symptoms the victim usually recovers quickly and completely from all three forms of the disease.

PNEUMONIC PLAGUE. Infection spreads to lungs causing pneumonia. Coughing expels millions of contagious bacteria. Sharp chest pains. Continuous fever. Heavy sweating. Spitting up of blood. Death within three days or less.

SEPTICAEMIC PLAGUE. Infection in bloodstream. Least common form of disease. Most fatal. Sudden severe illness. Chills, fever, headache, nausea, vomiting, delirium. No time for other symptoms to develop. Death within a few hours to two days.

This is how people at the time described the plague. Such descriptions are called contemporary accounts.

"*The victims died almost immediately. They would swell beneath their armpits and in their groins and fall over dead while talking.*"

Before the end "*death is seen seated on the face.*"

It seemed as if one sick person "*could infect the whole world.*"

"*Woe is me of the shilling on the armpit! It is seething, terrible . . . a head that gives pain and causes a loud cry . . . a painful angry knob . . . Great is it seething like a burning cinder.*"

Modern people know that infectious diseases:

- are caused by organisms such as bacteria and viruses from outside invading the body
- can be passed from one person to another
- usually raise the temperature of the victim or cause a fever.

Plague can be cured today because scientists have found out the bacteria that causes plague is carried by rats and the fleas that live on rats. The flea finds a rat to be its host. It bites the rat and infects the blood of the rat. When the flea or rat bites a human, it passes the disease on. When the human comes into contact with other humans, it passes the disease on.

But nobody in the Middle Ages knew this. People who wrote about the plague never mentioned fleas. They only mentioned rats in passing. Yet fleas and rats were common pests.

The plague bacillus was not discovered for another 500 years.

Robert Browning's famous poem, *'The Pied Piper of Hamelin'*, is the story of a plague of rats in the German town of Hamelin.

Rats!
They fought the dogs and killed the cats
And bit the babies in the cradles
And ate the cheeses out of the vats
And licked the soup from the cooks' own ladles
Split open the kegs of salted sprats
Made nests inside men's Sunday hats
And even spoiled the women's chats . . .

SKILL / PŪKENGA

Detective Work / Making Connections

Draw up four boxes like this:

Rats in general	Black rats	Brown rats	Fleas

Use the clues to sort these facts into the four boxes.

- are heavy breeders
- lay eggs in the hair of animals, in dirt and rubbish
- two most common types are the black rat and brown rat
- poison, gas and traps are ways of killing them
- jump as much as 200 times their body-length
- also called Roof and Climbing rats
- weigh about 200 grams
- feed on the blood of a host
- also called Sewer or Wharf rats
- dig and burrow and are good swimmers
- rodent, Rattus
- can feed on almost anything edible
- will often move from one host to another
- commonly found in cities, especially sea ports, in upper storeys of houses and buildings
- tend to stay near people
- fleas are very infectious
- weigh up to 450 grams
- can go without food for several months if necessary
- fleas are less infectious
- do not rely so much on people

CLUES

[1] The black rat is an excellent climber and jumper.
[2] The brown rat is bigger than the black rat.
[3] The black rat came to Europe during the Crusades before the Black Death.
[4] The brown rat came to Europe in trading ships in the 16th and 17th centuries.
[5] When the brown rat arrived, it began to replace the black rat.
[6] Black rats live in dry places and brown rats live close to water.

Answers are with Teacher's Photocopy Sheets

Working Out Relationships

1 Write a sentence about how the Black Death would have got its name.

2 There were reported cases of doctors catching the disease at a bedside and dying before the patient and of people going to bed well and dying before they woke up. Which are the two best words to describe such a disease – *inconsequential, merciful, virulent, demanding, lethal, flexible*?

3 Make a drawing to show the link between **flea, rat** and **human** in the plague chain.

4 Use the contemporary accounts to write a sentence about why depression and despair accompanied the physical symptoms of the disease.

THIS MUST BE PUNISHMENT FROM GOD

Medieval artists often drew the disease as an arrow

The Unscientific State of Medicine in 1347

- For the two centuries before the Black Death, there had been a great medical school at Salerno in Italy. It trained women doctors as well as men.
- Doctors were described as wealthy people. They wore red or purple gowns. They had belts of silver thread. Their hoods were furred. They had embroidered gloves. If they rode to visit a patient, they would wear golden spurs. A servant went with them.
- Quacks such as the Triacleurs who used treacle as a cure, visited fairs and markets. They sold useless pills and ointments and potions.
- Cures were a mixture of common-sense and superstition. Doctors set broken bones and pulled out rotten teeth. They made anaesthetics from opium and hemlock and used herbs such as dock for swollen glands and rue for nose bleeds. They took cataracts off eyes with a silver needle. A mixture of oil, vinegar and sulphur was used to treat toothache and ground peony root with oil of roses was a treatment for headaches. They applied a truss for a hernia. For ringworm they recommended washing the scalp with a boy's urine and for gout, a plaster of goat dung mixed with rosemary and honey was applied. To stop the pockmarks in a smallpox patient, they wrapped the patient in red cloth in a bed with red hangings.
- People thought that a cause of disease was too much blood in the body. So doctors put leeches on the sick person's body. The leeches fastened themselves on to the skin with their teeth and sucked out blood. This is why doctors were sometimes called *leeches*.
- Sick people went on visits to shrines. Sometimes the sick were carried long distances to places that were thought of as sacred.
- Often a sick child was weighed and the same weight of gold or silver was given to a shrine if the child recovered.
- Today we know that the plague is caused by bacteria. These organisms are so small you cannot see them without a microscope. People in the Middle Ages did not have microscopes. The microscope was not invented until about 1590. And bacteria were not discovered until about 1680. Even then another hundred years went by before it was suggested that bacteria might cause disease. But most scientists thought disease produced bacteria instead of the other way around. The plague disease had different forms. This confused medieval people even more. Their lack of scientific knowledge made them come up with other causes for the Black Death.

In 1348 the medical faculty at the University of Paris announced that the plague was caused by a triple conjunction of Saturn, Jupiter and Mars in the 40th degree of Aquarius that happened on March 20 1345. This had poisoned the surrounding air.

A big battle between planets and oceans made waters rise and vaporise. Fish died in masses and poisoned the air.

Wicked people have poisoned the wells where people get their drinking water.

Sheets of fire and huge rains of fire

The Hand of the Evil One has struck.

A Pest Maiden comes out of the mouths of dead people. It is like a blue flame. It flies through the air to spread disease to the next house.

Thick stinking mists

Clouds of poison

Foul blasts of wind from the seacoast

Strange tempests

People get ill when sick people look at them.

It is the wrath of God. People are being punished for their sins. God has sent the plague because people are sinning too much.

Black smoke

What people in 1347 thought caused the Black Death

Huge hailstones

Earthquakes let out foul fumes from inside the Earth.

Wicked people with bottles of poisoned air have opened the bottles and let the air escape.

Skill / Pūkenga

Working Out Relationships

Use the following contemporary comments to make a general statement about the relationship between medieval people and their religion.

- The mystery of the contagion is '*the most terrible of all the terrors.*' [Flemish cleric in Avignon]
- '*The pestilence with which God is afflicting the Christian people.*' [Pope in a Bull of September 1348]
- The plague is '*a chastisement from Heaven.*' [Emperor John Cantacuzene]
- '*The pestilences were for pure sin.*' [Piers Plowman, ploughman hero of a story]
- *At the beginning of October 1347, twelve Genoese galleys were fleeing from the vengeance which God was taking ... In their bones they bore so deadly an illness and could not avoid death. The infection then spread to anyone who met the diseased.*' [Franciscan Friar Michäel of Piazza]

Creative Writing

You are a nun or a monk. It is 1349. All the members of your community have died of the Black Death. You have had to bury them. Sometimes five bodies a day. Only a dog is left. Because you have had some education, you know how to write. You think you must leave a record of what has happened. So you find parchment, ink and a quill. You know that this might be the last thing you write. You have heard of other chroniclers dying in the middle of writing a sentence.

Write your record. To help get you started, read the following. It is by Petrarch, a famous Italian poet. On 19 May 1348, he wrote to his brother who was the only survivor of a convent of thirty five. This is what he said.

"My brother! My brother! Alas what shall I say? Whither shall I turn? On all sides is sorrow, everywhere is fear. I would that I had never been born, or, at least had died before these times. How will posterity believe that there has been a time, without lightnings of heaven or fires of Earth, without wars or other visible slaughter, not this or that part of the Earth, but well nigh the whole globe has remained without inhabitants? When before has it been seen that houses are left vacant, cities deserted, fields are too small for the dead, and a fearful and universal solitude over the whole Earth?"

PLAGUE VERSUS THE MEDIEVAL MIND

The medieval mind seems weird to you today because you have science to show you how disease works. But if you had caught the plague in the Middle Ages, you would not have had science to help you understand and fight your disease.

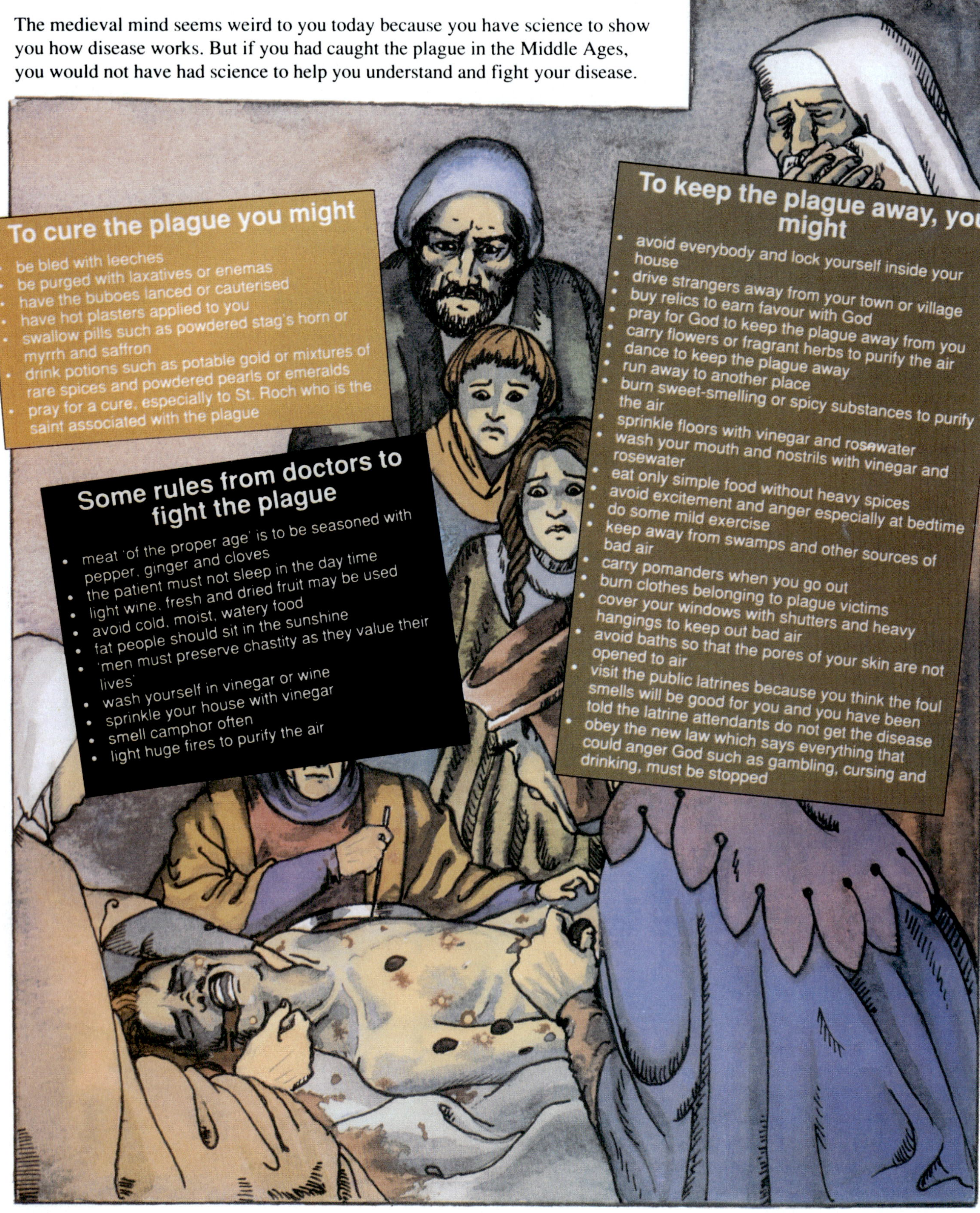

SKILL / PŪKENGA

Comparing Medieval and Modern Mind-sets

1 Find medieval methods of dealing with the plague that might be contradictory.

2 Find methods that would come under the general heading of *purification of the air.*

3 Even if a method worked, medieval people did not understand why. The Pope's doctor got the Pope to sit in his chambers between two roaring fires. This must have been hard in the summer heatwave. The Pope did not get the plague. The medieval explanation for this was that the fires had purified the air. What is a more likely explanation?

4 These are some things that may or may not help fight the plague. Put them into two lists, one list for the things medieval people would choose and one list for the things modern people would choose. Use your lists to prepare a statement about the two different mind-sets of medieval and modern people.

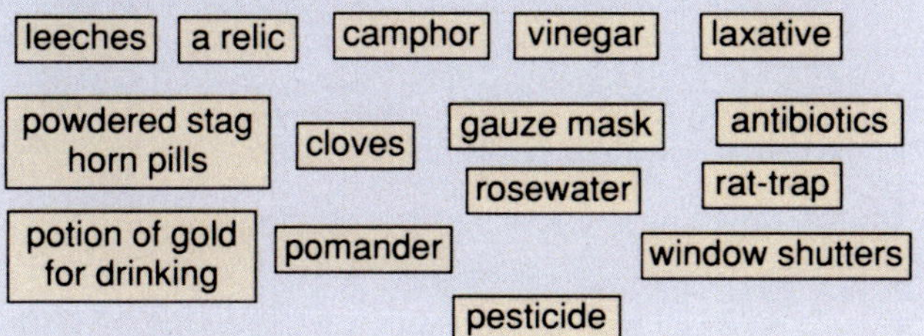

5 Role-playing a Character

Become someone who lives in a European town in 1348. Give yourself a name. Some ideas for characters follow this.

Choose the methods you use to try to stay alive. Decide how well these methods work, whether or not you become infected with plague and what your fate is. Present your character to your group.

Some Ideas for Characters

- Wealthy person who is terrified of plague.
- Villager living in a hovel.
- Quack who sells dirty water as a magic cure.
- Priest who refuses to hear confessions from the dying.
- Lord who wants to burn the peasants' village down because plague has arrived in it.
- Merchant who is marooned outside his city's gates because of quarantine.
- Ruler who ordered plague houses to be walled up with everybody, dead and alive, still inside.
- Flagellant in a group travelling through the town.

THE FLAGELLANTS – A WAYOUT REACTION

During the time of the Black Death, people called flagellants stripped to the waist and whipped themselves until they bled. They used leather whips tipped with iron spikes. They thought this could make up for human wickedness. It might make God take the Black Death away. They cried out to Christ and the Virgin for pity. They asked God to spare them from the disease.

Usually there were about two to three hundred people in a group of flagellants. They were not all poor peasants. Some knights and ladies and clergy and nuns and children joined too. They walked from place to place and performed in church squares. People in the towns and villages greeted them by ringing church bells. They invited the flagellants to stay in their houses. Sometimes they brought children to the flagellants to be healed. They dipped cloths in the blood from the flagellants and pressed the cloths to their own eyes. They kept the cloths as relics.

A Master organised each group. To become a flagellant, you would agree to work for 33 and a half days. Can you work out why that time limit was chosen? You were not allowed to do things like change your clothes, wash yourself or sleep in a bed without the Master's permission. The women had to stay at the back of the procession. If a woman or a priest entered the circle of the performance, it had to start again.

The Masters claimed they could hear confession. Priests who tried to stop them were stoned. The flagellants took over churches and interrupted services. They claimed they could cast out evil spirits and bring the dead to life again.

The church and leaders finally tried to stop the flagellants. They locked them out of towns. They passed laws that threatened death for public flagellation. Most of the flagellants had disappeared by the time the Black Death had passed.

THE IMPACT OF THE DISEASE

SKILL / PŪKENGA

Using Primary Sources to Explore Values

Primary sources are writings by people who were alive at the time. They are valuable although they do not always give a full picture. During the time of the Black Death, the people who could write were the wealthy and educated. There are no records from poor peasants. And although the chroniclers might have been seeing cartload after cartload of corpses go past their window as they were writing, they had no way of counting the number of bodies. The Black Death was something they would never have imagined in their worst nightmares. This may have coloured their accounts.

A hypothesis is an idea or a theory. If you make a hypothesis you are making a suggestion that you can use as a starting point for finding out an answer. An example is – '*I think the Black Death killed so many people it would have made the survivors* . . . . . (sad? happy? unbalanced? determined to lead better lives?)'.

Values are standards on which you base your actions or beliefs. The attitudes of people towards other people during the Black Death shows some of their values. An example of a statement of values is – '*During the Black Death, the attitude of people towards each other was one of* .... (caring? not caring? helpful? not helpful?)'

1 Make a hypothesis for this question – '*What was the state of mind of people in Europe as the Black Death killed their family, relations, friends, clergy and doctors?*'

2 Then read the primary sources for information that might help you develop or change your hypothesis.

3 Rework your hypothesis as a statement. In your statement include a comment about values.

Designing a Game

Design a computer or a card game about the way medieval people reacted to the plague. Try to include these –

- **a** a mock-up or model of some part of the game
- **b** rules how to play
- **c** description of what age and how many players the game is suitable for
- **d** your aim in designing the game (what you hope people playing it will get out of it)
- **e** the name of the game
- **f** a plan for a television or newspaper advertisement for the game

And no bells tolled and nobody wept no matter what his loss because almost everyone expected death.

Men and women . . . wandered around as if mad.

Whenever one or two people died in any house, at once, or at least in a short space of time, the rest of the household were carried off. So much so, that very often in one home ten or more ended their lives together, and in many houses, the dogs and even cats died. Hence no one, whether rich or poor, was secure, but everyone, from day to day, waited on the will of the Lord.

My boy Nanni was stricken and in a day and a half we buried him. In Florence the destruction fills one with pity.

Daily, some rich man is borne by these ruffians to his burial, without lights, without a friend to follow him. All in the streets fly when his body approaches. Nor do these wretched gavoti, strong as they are, escape. Most of them after a time become infected by the contagion and die.

God is deaf now-a-days and deigneth not hear us,
And prayers have no power the Plague to stay.

And people said and believed 'This is the end of the world'.

In this extremity of our city's sufferings . . . the authority of laws was abused and all but totally dissolved, for lack of those who should have administered and enforced them, most of whom, like the rest of the citizens were either dead or sick.

Many died daily or nightly in the public streets . . . It was the common practice of most of the neighbours . . . to drag the corpses out of the houses with their own hands, and lay them round in front of the doors.

There was no one who wept for any death, for all awaited death.

Citizen avoided citizen, so among neighbours was scarce found any that showed fellow-feeling for another.

And no one could be found to bury the dead for money or friendship . . . and I, Agnola di Tura, called The Fat, buried my five children with my own hands, and so did many others likewise.

Primary sources of reactions to the Black Death

The whole world, as it were, placed within the grasp of the Evil One . . . I leave parchment to continue this work, if perchance any man survive and any of the race of Adam escape this pestilence and carry on the work which I have begun.

He spent himself caring for the sick until he fell ill from too constant attendance on them. He lived six days and died. I, Francis of Folignio was present at his illness and did not leave him until death.

And in these days was burying without sorrowe and wedding without friendschippe.

A father did not visit his son, nor his son his father. Charity was dead.

How many grand palaces, how many stately homes . . . once full of retainers, of lords, of ladies . . . were now left empty of all.

Father abandoned child, wife husband, one brother another for this plague seemed to strike through the breath and sight. And so they died.

So few servants and labourers were left that no one knew where to turn for help.

The nuns, having no fear of death, tended the sick with all sweetness and humility.

Only the stench of their bodies informed neighbours of their death.

They forgot the past as though it had never been and gave themselves up to a more disordered and shameful life than they had led before.

Corpses were abandoned in empty houses and there was none to give them Christian burial.

The care of those stricken fell to the Friars Minor and members of other orders whose convents were soon emptied of their inhabitants.

Oh happy posterity who will not experience such abysmal woe and will look upon our testimony as a fable.

It was a cruel and horrible thing; and I do not know where to begin to tell of the cruelty and the pitiless ways. It seemed to almost everyone that one became stupified by seeing the pain.

I will not write of the cruelty that there was in the countryside, of the wolves and wild beasts that ate the poorly buried corpses, and of other cruelties that would be too painful to those who read of them.

The plague waxes in various places and spreads in this direction . . . People are much afraid and the deaths are beginning . . . In God's name we will send you our boy Pippo.

Members of a household brought their dead to a ditch as best they could, without priest, without divine offices. Nor did the death bell sound.

The malady seemed to set at naught both the art of the physician and the virtues of physic . . . Some people consulted quacks, for there was now a multitude of both men and women who practised without having received the slightest tincture of medical science.

Magistrates and notaries refused to come and make the wills of the dying . . . Even the priests did not come to hear their confessions.

And so many died that all believed that it was the end of the world.

Priests turned away from the care of their benefices from fear of death.

One man shunned another . . . kinsfolk held aloof, brother was forsaken by brother, oftentimes husband by wife, nay, what is more, and scarcely to be believed, fathers and mothers were found to abandon their own children to their fate, untended, unvisited as if they had been strangers.

Seeing what a calamity of sudden death had come to them by the arrival of the Genoese, the people of Messina drove them in all haste from their city and port.

No one had any inclination to concern themselves about the future.

And in that time the mortality was so great among the people of Normandy that those of Picardy mocked them.

Then the father abandoned the sick son; magistrates and notaries refused to come and make the wills of the dying.

LET'S BLAME THE JEWS

SUMMARY FACT
Jews were hated and persecuted during the time of the plague.

Attacks on the Jews in Europe begin after people start to die of the plague. They last until the end of 1349.

The Jews are accused of poisoning the wells so they can destroy the Christians and become lords of the world.

- The charges say messengers from Toledo carried poison in little packets and leather bags and brought instructions for sprinkling the poison into wells and springs.
- Confessions are got by torture.

Narbonne/Carcassonne (Spring 1348)
Jews are dragged from their houses and thrown into bonfires.

Savoy (September 1348)
Formal trials held. Eleven Jews are burned alive. The others have to pay taxes to be allowed to stay in city.

Basle (January 1349)
Several hundred Jews are burned in a specially built wooden house.

Strassbourg (February 1349)
Two thousand Jews are taken to burial grounds. Those who refuse to convert are burned at rows of stakes.

Worms (March 1349)
Jewish community burn themselves to death inside their own houses rather than be killed.

Mainz (August 1349)
Jews rise up against the mob after them and kill. Then they retreat to their homes and set fire to them. It is thought six thousand die.

Frankfurt-Am-Main (July 1349)
Jewish community burn themselves to death inside their own houses rather than be killed.

Antwerp/Brussels (December 1349)
The whole Jewish community is wiped out.

The Jews Were Different

Medieval people did not know about bacteria or the antibiotics that are needed to control them. They believed that God was punishing them by sending the Black Death. But they could not attack God. So they looked around for something else they could blame and attack. The Jews were an obvious target because they were different in many ways to Christians.

- Jews were thought of as strangers. Jews had separated themselves from the Christian church.
- For centuries Christians had been taught to hate the Jews.
- Christians thought the Jews hated them too and wanted to harm them.
- Laws had stopped Jews from doing crafts or trades. So they had been pushed into money-lending. They had been allowed to do this because kings always needed money. Christians looked down on money-lenders. They thought the Jews were making fortunes.
- Jews lived in a group of their own kind in a particular street or quarter. Jews were called 'outcasts'.
- Jews were called 'Christ-killers'.
- Rumours said that Jews kidnapped and tortured Christian children and drank their blood to make themselves look human.
- Jews had not been allowed to own land. This was another thing that made them different.
- Jews had property that could be looted.
- People were used to blaming diseases on well-poisoning by lepers or other groups of people.
- The church had made rules such as Jews were not allowed to hire Christians as servants or serve as doctors to Christians.
- Laws passed by countries said Jews had to show they were Jewish. They might not be allowed to cut their hair. They might have to wear yellow cone-shaped hats. Or special tabards. These marked the Jews out as being different in the various countries in which they lived.
- Jews were said to warn their families and other Jews not to drink from certain wells and springs.
- It was said that all Jews over the age of seven were guilty as they knew about the poisonings of wells.

In September 1348, Pope Clement VI issued a Bull about the Jews. It said.

- Christians who blamed Jews for the plague had been seduced by the devil
- the charge of well-poisoning and the massacres of the Jews were horrible
- the plague was killing all people including Jews
- the plague was in places where no Jews were living
- the clergy should take Jews under their protection.

Skill / Pūkenga

Developing Ideas

1 Read the Summary Fact and then the information underneath which supports the Summary Fact.

2 In groups develop ideas for why Jews have been hated and persecuted many times through history.

3 Decide how many of your ideas would be right for the time of the Black Death by reading the information about why the Jews were thought of as different and therefore good targets for people looking for someone to blame for the Black Death.

Creating a Story Outline for a Movie

Your group wants funding to make a movie about a fourteen year old Jewish girl or boy accused of well poisoning in 1348. To apply for the funding, you have to present an outline of your movie. The outline should include –

1 A brief summary of the plot.

2 The list of cast for the movie.

3 The names of people in your group and their specialist jobs.

4 A list of problems you think could come up during filming and ideas you have for preventing or fixing those problems.

5 A newspaper advertisement for your film, saying what audience it is suitable for and why people should go to see it.

6 Reasons why you think it is important for New Zealanders today to see a movie about an event that happened in Europe so long ago.

THE BLACK DEATH DISORGANISED SOCIETY

When the graveyards were full, bodies were thrown into rivers. Families put their relatives into pits or buried them so quickly that dogs dug them up. Reports everywhere spoke of the sick dying too fast for the living to bury. Corpses lay in the streets for days at a time. People had no energy to take them away.

A group of people talking about the disorganisation of society after the Black Death . . .

"Young Wat's done alright. Only one left in his family. Inherits the lot."

"Squire bought a horse this morning. Worth forty shillings before the pestilence. Squire got it for six shillings."

"Prices gone crazy. Who'd ever guessed we'd afford silk to wear and fancy plate to eat off?"

"You wait. Soon as all the cheap stuff's gone, prices will go up again. Real high."

"Cattle and sheep wandering all over the place. Mucking up crops. Lost property. Finder's keeper's."

"Don't matter much. Crops are rotting in the fields."

"Can't stomach this change in fashion I see in town. Those new rich think they've got to show it off."

"Old gentry at least had some manners. This new lot's rough and rude."

"Hear a lot of town poor have shifted into the rich houses. Ones left empty from the disease."

"Be a lot of houses go to ruin now. Wages so high, people won't afford repairs."

"Saw that priest the other day. Different now they've let ordinary men deal to the dying, hear confession and all. I heard they even let some women do that. Priest won't be able to threaten me any more when I don't go to his church."

"Lot of priests charged huges fees. Refused to go to the dying. Let Christians die with no sacraments."

"Church's even richer now though. Lot of people left all their money to it."

"Seems like now all anyone's interested in is having a good time. Gambling and drinking. Sinning worse than ever. Priests just as bad. Even monks and nuns."

"People reckon they've got it made because they cheated death."

"Hear the next village, everyone died at the castle. Peasants went in and took everything."

"Bad there. Got women and little kids out ploughing. Not enough men left."

"Lot of strikes in town now. People wanting better wages. Hardly any workers left."

"That new statute they passed, Statute of Labourers they call it. Trying to make everyone work for the same pay as 1347."

Nobody knows exactly how many people died of the Black Death. Some of the contemporary reports seem unreliable. For example some chroniclers said 62,000 people died in Avignon and others said 120,000 people died there. But the total population of Avignon was probably less than 50,000 to start with.

Any figures are just estimates. It is estimated, for example, that in 1347 the population of London was 70,000. It is estimated that 30,000 Londoners died from the plague in 1348 and 1349. What percentage of people is that?

Modern demographers think Froissart was right when he wrote that 'a third of the world died.' They think that a third of Europe was probably about 20 million deaths. Nothing else had killed so many people in such a short space of time.

"You get caught breaking that, you could end up in prison. You run away, you're an outlaw. They reckon they'll brand an F on your forehead. Fugitive."

"How about those vagrancy laws they got now? You want to beg, you got to wear a special badge. Get a licence. Renew it every six months."

"People jumbled up all over the place. Villages deserted. New people in towns."

"Good chance for new jobs. Maybe set up a business. Clerk gets to be a merchant. Farm labourer a gentleman farmer."

"Bad news for Government. They're giving jobs to anyone who can read half a word. Not an honest person in sight."

"Half the town's running off to fortune-tellers. Other half's listening to madmen."

"Squire's turning land over to sheep. Wages are too high. Not enough labourers. But even with the sheep, won't be able to stop some of the land going back wild."

"Good for our rents though. Squire's dropped them for a year. He's that desperate for labour."

"Marriage rate's gone up. Not for love though. Lot of orphan brides. Rich dowries."

"Lawsuits all over the place. Trying to sort out properties. Not enough lawyers left to cope."

"Not enough clergy left to teach boys their grammar."

"All that knowledge just gone. But they're setting up more universities."

"Hear over the seas they've hiked up the taxes. Less people to pay them. Made people wild."

"Everyone's nerves are shot."

"I reckon people are all scared. Gloomy. Depressed. Nobody trusts anyone now."

"Some weird things going on. How about that dancing mania. You join hands in a circle, they say. Go into frenzies. Foam at the mouth. Fall down exhausted."

"It's called tarantism. Supposed to get it from bites of tarantula spider."

"Things will never be the same again. Peasants are all stirred up about their conditions. Made them realise they can demand better. Be a revolt soon."

SKILL / PŪKENGA

Finding Possible Reasons for Events

What reasons can you suggest for the following events?

1 During the Black Death, a pack of wolves came down from the Austrian Alps to prey upon sheep that were lying dead in the fields. But suddenly the wolves turned and fled back into the wilderness.

2 Women appeared to get the disease more quickly than men.

3 Milliners and dress-makers did well from the Black Death.

4 The Scots thought that while the English were stricken with the plague, it was a good time to attack the English. They crossed the border but their plans backfired.

5 King Alfonso X1 of Castile was the only reigning monarch to be killed by the Black Death.

6 The death rate from the Black Death was high among doctors and clergy.

7 Rich people fled into the countryside during the Black Death.

8 Most cities stopped funeral bells ringing and criers announcing deaths during the Black Death.

9 Most cities limited the number going to a funeral to two people during the Black Death.

10 During the Black Death, work stopped on the cathedral being built in Siena. The cathedral was planned to be the biggest in the world. Work never started on it again.

Making Up and Putting on a Play

Your group's challenge is to put on a play about a group of young people talking about the impact of the Black Death.

Use the dialogue in the box to help you get started. You could add to it and put it into more modern or more old-fashioned language.

Plague 20th Century Style

Plague has never died out in the world. And neither have rats. In some countries they are a big pest. Not just undeveloped countries either. In 1995 Britain found that it had 60 million rats. That meant more rats than people there. In London alone, 300,000 properties were infested with rats. The increase was blamed on the rats' resistance to poison, the milder weather and the growing fast-food industry with its throw-away rubbish. Scientists warned that the rats were a threat to people because they could spread disease.

Skill / Pūkenga

New Zealand's Plague Scare

1 1900 Bubonic plague breaks out in Sydney. 116 cases and 40 deaths among them are reported. A case is reported in Auckland. This is part of a world pandemic.

2 1900 The Bubonic Plague Prevention Act gives the Governor 'full and absolute power to direct, require and enforce any matter which in his absolute discretion he thinks expedient in order to promptly and effectively deal with the bubonic plague.'

3 In suspect districts of Auckland, residents are cleared out of their homes and put in quarantine. Their belongings, including things like sewing machines and pianos, are drenched with disinfectant and whitewash. A lot of slums are pulled down without notice to the occupants.

4 1901 Department of Public Health is set up to centralise public health measures.

5 The *New Zealand Observer* says – 'Epidemics of disease may be bad, but it is more than possible that they are not worse than epidemics of inspectors. This latter seems to be our worst plague at the present time. As the Hon. W. Jennings said in the Legislative Council the other day, every vestige of the people's liberty is being destroyed by this Health Department. And our trouble is not with health inspectors alone. Nowadays, we have inspectors to see that hens lay eggs of the right colour, inspectors to punish people for allowing Scotch thistles to grow in their gardens, and inspectors for everything else under the sun. And all the inspectors draw fat salaries from the people whom they are paid to oppress.'

6 1900 An Aucklander dies of plague. 1902 Three of four reported Auckland victims die. Victim in Lyttelton dies. 1911 One of eight Auckland victims die. Plague disappears.

Recognising Different Reactions to an Event

1 Which box contains more opinions than other boxes?

2 Which box contains a lot of jargon and legal language?

3 Which box contains a reaction at the grassroots level?

4 Which box contains a reaction at the parliamentary level?

5 Which box would a demographer be most interested in?

6 Which box shows the plague was in other countries as well as New Zealand?

PLAGUE IN INDIA

Plague has hit India hard. In the pandemic of the 1890s, more than 1 million people in India died. In outbreaks between 1949 and 1959, 59,000 people died. Then in 1994 plague struck India again.

First it was bubonic plague in the Beed district of India which is 300 km southeast of Bombay. Health authorities gave out Tetracycline capsules. They sprayed with insecticides. Tribesmen were brought in to catch rats.

Then pneumonic plague broke out in the city of Surat. It is 250 km north of Bombay. Two million people live in this polluted industrial city. There is little sanitation. A lot of people sleep in the streets. Garbage piles up. Recent floods had left a lot of animal carcasses about.

Thousands of plague cases were reported in Surat. The death toll started to climb. Shops, offices, schools and cinemas closed. People wrapped scarves round their heads to protect themselves. Hundreds of thousands of people fled from the city. Some were private doctors and nurses and other health aides. A lot of them headed for Bombay.

The plague spread to other places. Neighbouring countries began to close their land borders and stop air connections. Other countries posted medical watches at airports. Eventually the plague tailed off.

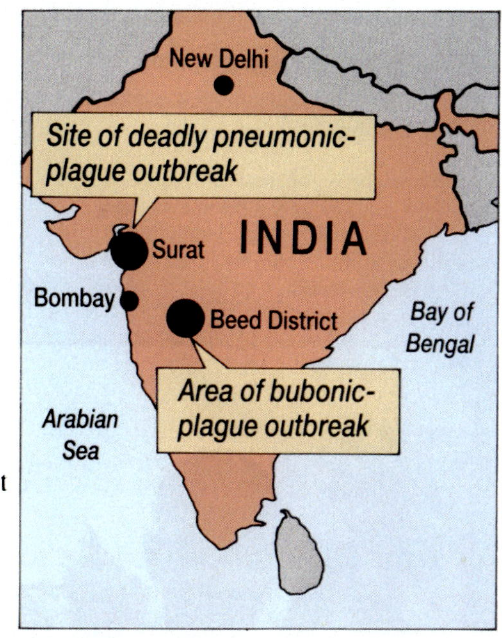

SKILL / PŪKENGA

Preparing a Feature Article

It is India 1994. The editor of a newspaper in Surat has invited you to do a feature on the recent plague outbreak from the point of view of young people. You have already interviewed a lot of students and summarised some of their comments (see the quotes in the boxes). Prepare your feature. It should include:

- an eye-catching headline
- at least one illustration
- a sketch map
- an explanation of other people's opinions and why different people have different opinions.

The local authorities should be sued for the pollution and mess in this city. [Hasita]

Our cities are so polluted they probably harbour all sorts of epidemics like the plague. [Sama]

My fever went down quite quickly but my joints ached for days. [Nata]

The official reaction was shameful. It was like putting a sticking plaster over something that needed major surgery. [Priya]

Why did so many people run away? Did they think war had broken out? [Rama]

My brother got it. We were worried sick. But at least nowadays they've got antibiotics. [Devi]

Sure, a lot of people died. But there were wild rumours of people dying like flies. [Hasin]

The organisation in the city is awful. Too many people for not enough facilities. [Vijay]

It was like what we'd learned at school about the Black Death was happening here. [Veda]

How could they have stopped people leaving? Built a wall? Put sharpshooters on it? [Patu]

The politicians only think about the next elections. [Uma]

My father said it wasn't rats but the media that spread the disease. [Varun]

It's given the world a bad image of India. [Chandra]

I hope this epidemic will make the authorities in this city wake up and start to clean up. [Amin]

They should be ashamed they can put people on the moon yet not get rid of the plague. [Karma]

I've never seen such panic in my life. People just lost it. [Syed]

SKILL / PŪKENGA

Understanding Photographs

1 For each photograph, give a title and a caption.

2 There are no photos of plague in Europe in 1347 because the camera had not been invented. Discuss the idea that a photo can say more than a thousand words.

D

THE GREAT FLU EPIDEMIC IN NEW ZEALAND

The influenza epidemic of 1918 was the worst pandemic since the Black Death of 1347. It killed more than 21 million people around the world. About 9 million people had been killed in the First World War of 1914-18.

Nobody knows the exact figure for how many people in New Zealand the influenza killed. Estimates range from 6,500 to 8,500. The whole population of New Zealand at that time was not much more than 500,000.

People called it the Plague of the Spanish Lady because of the damage it did in Spain. Or Black Flu because the victims sometimes turned black after they had died. This made people think of the Black Death.

It began in Europe in April 1918. It spread rapidly and then went to Asia and the United States and then to Australasia. It hit New Zealand when people were getting ready to put their lives back to normal after the war.

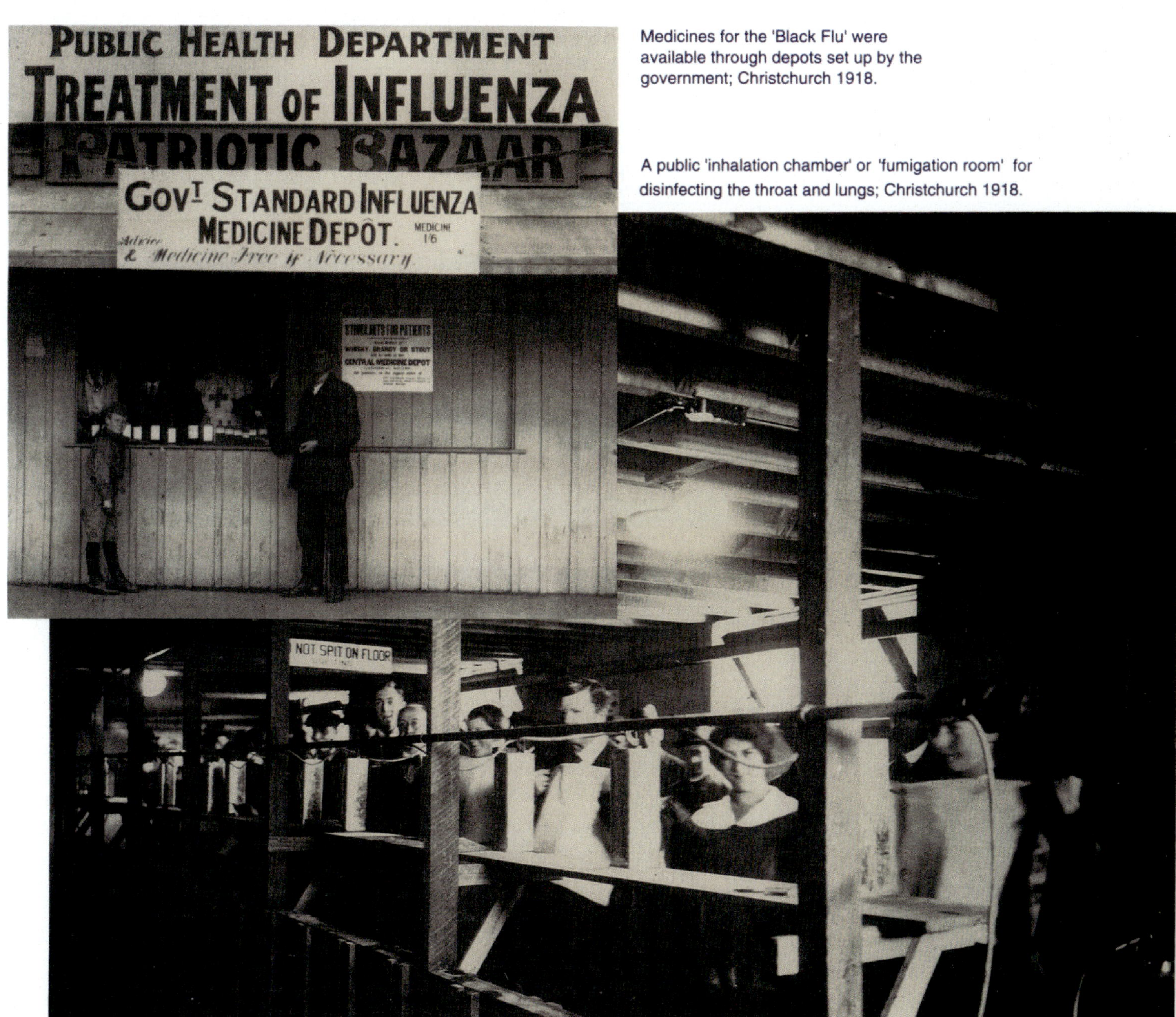

Medicines for the 'Black Flu' were available through depots set up by the government; Christchurch 1918.

A public 'inhalation chamber' or 'fumigation room' for disinfecting the throat and lungs; Christchurch 1918.

Putting Events in Order

To put events in order you have to be a detective. Use the words underlined in each box to show your order.

CLUES
- Although a Royal Commission says later that *SS Niagara* brought the disease to New Zealand, it was already here before the ship arrived.
- Arguments over quarantine for ships had started before the *SS Niagara* arrived.

How the epidemic began

12 October *SS Niagara* is a day out from Auckland. Ship sends a message that it has influenza cases. NZ Prime Minister and Minister of Finance are on board.

The wireless message sent by the master of the *SS Niagara* to the Auckland port authorities –

"Please advise Health Department Spanish influenza cases on board; increasing daily. Present time over 100 crew down. Urgently required hospital assistance and accommodation for 25 serious cases. Arriving schedule."

After the first deaths from the *SS Niagara*, the first fumigation room opens in Auckland.

Epidemic becomes more severe in other parts of the country.

Reports start of influenza epidemic in Auckland and in military camps at Trentham and Featherston and in Wellington.

In Auckland *SS Niagara* passes disease onto another steamer which takes it to Samoa. Disease has one of highest hit rates in the world in Samoa.

11 November World War 1 ends. New Zealanders celebrate.

Two patients from *SS Niagara* die in hospital. Other deaths follow. People start to speak of "the plague".

Argument about quarantine for ships coming to New Zealand infected with influenza. Suggestion made to Minister for Public Health that infected ships be isolated and fumigated.

Minister for Public Health clears *SS Niagara* for landing in Auckland. Patients from ship are put in hospital.

Third week of November. Disease peaks.

End of December. Disease dies away

An influenza fumigation centre; 1919.

MORE DEAD FROM FLU

Thirteen deaths from influenza occurred in Auckland yesterday. Twelve more Auckland Hospital nurses and two more junior medical officers have been stricken with the complaint.

A large number of applications for admission were received at the hospital but the majority had to be refused owing to lack of accommodation.

A notice issued by the acting chief health officer, Dr J. P. Frengley, requires the immediate closing of all schools, theatres, public halls, billiard rooms, shooting galleries and other places of entertainment. This will include the Auckland Racing Club's course and buildings at Ellerslie and means that no races can be held on Saturday.

Over 300 persons submitted themselves to treatment at the precautionary steam spray inhalation chamber at the Public Health Department.

NZ Herald November 5 1918

Epidemics cause changes to society. Some are temporary. Some are more long-lasting. These are some of the changes that the influenza epidemic made in New Zealand.

More school nurses were appointed to teach children basic hygiene.

People turned to traditional folk remedies such as treacle and camphor bags.

A new Health Act was passed in 1920. The Health Department was given a face-lift.

It left a lot of solo parents. The war had already left a lot of widows.

Coal production from mines slowed down.

Improvements such as electricity and sewerage were made to housing.

Maori leaders such as Ratana and Princess Te Puea emphasised hygiene such as better water supply.

In some places the trams stopped running.

Trams, trains, trucks and carts were used as hearses.

White flags were put on mail-boxes to show there were dead bodies to be collected by the volunteers.

Because a lot of doctors were still away at war and many of the remaining doctors and nurses got sick, organisations such as Red Cross, St. John Ambulance and Voluntary Aid Detachments did the work.

Senior medical students helped nurse patients.

Children looked after sick relatives.

Many hotels, theatres and places of public entertainment closed.

Full hospitals had to turn patients away.

Children had more responsibility.

A Royal Commission was appointed. It said

- the *SS Niagara* had probably brought the disease to New Zealand
- New Zealand should improve its quarantine
- slums should be got rid of
- more attention in schools should be given to domestic science, hygiene, first aid and home nursing.

Minister of Public Health gave out special certificates to volunteers who worked in the epidemic as thanks from the Government.

People wore gauze face masks when dealing with the sick.

Doctors found many people knew nothing about basic hygiene or how infectious diseases spread.

Private cars were used as ambulances.

Inhalation chambers or fumigation rooms were set up. The spray was zinc-sulphate solution. The idea was to kill the influenza bugs. But some people said this could cause the influenza.

Alcohol was used to reduce the temperature and keep up the strength of the patient. At medicine depots, wall posters said 'Medicine supplied only to poor people with actual bad cases in the house' and 'Stimulants for patients – small bottles of whisky, brandy or stout.'

Some schools were closed and shops were shut.

SKILL / PŪKENGA

Thinking About the Impact of a Disease

1 Make one list of temporary results of the influenza epidemic and a second list of more permanent results.

2 Design a certificate that could be used for the Government to give to volunteer workers during the epidemic.

3 Question for discussion – Should the passengers from the *SS Niagara* have been allowed to come ashore without quarantine?
Prepare some ideas on this.

4 Read the newspaper article on page 28. Then make up a Public Notice in the form of a poster that could have appeared in the newspaper beside the article. The notice is from the Department of Health. The aim of the notice is to give advice about how to deal with the disease.

You might like to include some of these pieces of advice that people were given in 1918 –

- isolate the patient in a bright, well-ventilated room with no draughts
- only nurses or attendants are to enter the room; they must wear masks and use disinfectants
- the patient is not allowed outside for seven days, and not allowed in public for 14 days
- mild cases; gargle three times a day with salt and borax
- use pieces of rag for sputum then burn them
- serious cases should have plenty of light drinks and stimulants such as brandy or whisky every four hours and a hot sponge twice a day under a blanket
- extreme cases should have no stimulants but ice should be sucked, a hot water bottle should be placed on the feet and a doctor called for at once.

First published 1996, reprinted with updates 2004

Resources versus Killer Diseases

Bizarre theories

Virus turns flesh to pulp

Bodies abandoned for fear of virus

Virus spawns camp for Ebola refugees

Ebola pushes prices up, cuts flow of food

Virus hunters trap animals

EBOLA FEAR IN KINSHASA

Diamond hunter initial victim of killer virus

Nature's revenge for the destruction of Africa's rainforest?

Examples of Modern Epidemics

Aids (Acquired Immune Deficiency Syndrome)

- first reported in US in 1981 and now a major worldwide epidemic
- caused by the human immunodeficiency virus (HIV)
- by killing or harming cells of the immune system, HIV destroys the body's ability to fight infections and certain cancers so victims are in danger from life-threatening diseases called opportunistic infections, which are caused by microbes that usually do not cause illness in healthy people
- illnesses show as symptoms such as fever, fatigue, night sweats, loss of appetite, swollen lymph glands, weight loss, yeast infection, diarrhoea, dry mouth, rashes, headache, dry cough, memory and movement problems
- although there is no cure, some drugs slow the pace of infection
- HIV is spread by direct contact with infected body fluids, including blood, semen, vaginal secretion and breast milk; this means HIV in one of these fluids must get into the bloodstream by direct entry into a vein, a break in the skin or through mucous linings (other body fluids such as urine, saliva, vomit do not pose a risk unless visible blood is present; nor do mosquito bites)
- HIV is not easily transmissible (not transmitted through sneezing, coughing, eating or drinking from common utensils or being around a person with HIV; not transmitted through air, water, food or casual contact such as shaking hands, hugging, or use of restrooms and drinking fountains)
- no country is unaffected by Aids but getting help if you have Aids differs from country to country e.g. many victims in Africa are too poor to get drugs, lack education to know much about the disease, and have governments who are often slow to act (some leaders refused to accept that HIV was linked to Aids).

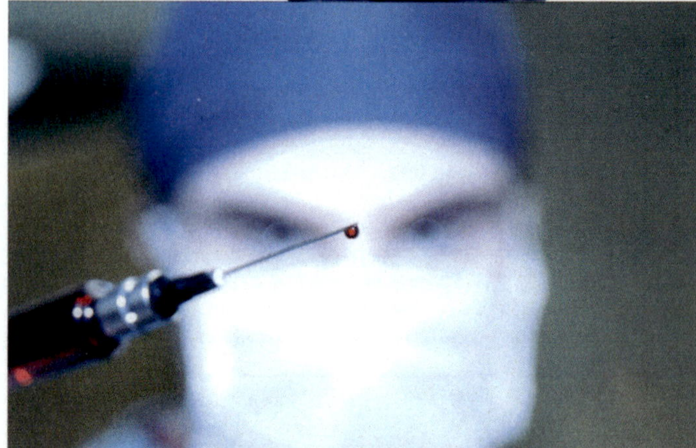

Avian influenza (Bird flu)

- does not usually make wild birds sick, but can kill domesticated birds
- normally does not infect humans; however, infections and outbreaks in humans have been reported since 1997 such as outbreaks in Hong Kong and the Netherlands which killed both chickens and humans
- millions of chickens have been slaughtered during outbreaks to remove the source of the virus
- spreads mainly from birds to humans, though there is rare person-to-person infection
- symptoms in humans range from typical flu-like symptoms (e.g., fever, cough, sore throat, muscle aches) to eye infections, pneumonia, acute respiratory distress, viral pneumonia
- no specific treatment; scientists continue to search for vaccines
- because it does not commonly infect humans, there is little or no immune protection in humans so if an avian virus were able to infect people and gain the ability to spread easily from person to person, a pandemic could begin.

Ebola Haemorrhagic Fever (EHF)

- one of the most deadly viral diseases known (kills 50-90% of all cases)
- named for river in Zaire, Africa, where it was first seen, in 1976
- since then there have been many outbreaks of it in Africa and the virus was found in monkeys in quarantine labs in the US.
- incubation is 2 to 21 days after infection
- symptoms are high fever, weakness, chills, headaches, pains, sore throat, loss of appetite, vomiting, hiccups, red and itchy eyes, diarrhea, rash, failure of blood to clot; bleeding (from eyes, lips, ears, nose, gums, skin)
- spreads through sexual contact, or hypodermic needles being reused on patients
- no specific treatment or vaccine.

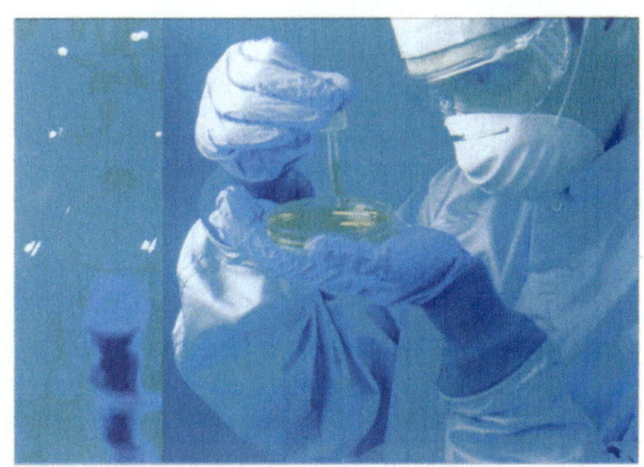

SARS (Severe Acute Respiratory Syndrome)

- viral respiratory illness first reported in Asia in 2003 from where it spread to more than two dozen countries before it was contained (hundreds died)
- symptoms include high fever, headache, overall feeling of discomfort, body aches, diarrhea, dry cough, pneumonia
- spread by close person-to-person contact e.g. when an infected person coughs or sneezes, or when a person touches something contaminated with infectious droplets and then touches his or her mouth, nose, or eye(s)
- incubation period is 2 to 14 days
- treatment is quarantine; scientists continue to search for vaccines.

SKILL / PŪKENGA

Use the data and pictures on pages 30 and 31 to help you prepare ideas and notes for discussion on the following questions about modern epidemics:

1. What are the names of some modern epidemics?
2. In what ways do these epidemics make challenges and crises for people?
3. What groups of people are trained to help during these epidemics?
4. How do people work together to deal with epidemics?
5. How has technology exposed modern cultures to epidemics from other places?
6. What is it like living through an epidemic?
7. What are some different causes of epidemics?
8. How are epidemics linked through cause and effect?
9. What are some past and likely future results of epidemics?
10. What groups of people have experienced particular epidemics?
11. How does an epidemic impact on people's lives in different ways?
12. Why do different groups sometimes experience epidemics differently?
13. What economic factors can decide the help people get during epidemics?
14. What social factors can decide the help people get during epidemics?
15. How does the access of people to help during epidemics affect their lives?
16. How could less advantaged groups get more help during epidemics?

THE IMPACT OF DISEASES

Epidemics can cause Governments to make changes in their health systems. An example is cholera in England. Until a century ago, thousands of people died from cholera each year in England. Once a single infected well near Piccadilly Circus in London killed almost 300 people in ten days. It was the closing of this well that led to the development of public health measures in Great Britain.

Epidemics can show how superstition is alive and well in societies. An example is a theory that Ebola got to Zaire in 1995 when a man came back sick from an illegal diamond-mining adventure. He swallowed a priceless diamond to fool people into believing it was lost. Doctors at the hospital cut him open and took the diamond out. He died. His father was angry. He went to witchdoctors who brought the disease on the hospital.

Epidemics can make individuals more aware. An example is the way each winter people in New Zealand are advised to be prepared to fight flu. The last new pandemic strain of influenza was the Hong Kong flu in 1969. In New Zealand the death rate was estimated at 76 for every hundred thousand. The usual flu death rate is about 20 per hundred thousand.

Epidemics can uncover ignorance. An example is the flu epidemic of 1918 in New Zealand which showed a lot of people did not know much about basic hygiene.

When epidemics start killing, people become desperate for explanations. An example is the wrath of God theory to explain the Black Death in Europe.

THE IMPACT OF DISEASES

Disease often becomes an important part of a country's folk history. An example is the stories about iron lungs from polio epidemics that are passed down through families.

Epidemics can change relationships among women, men and children. An example is the way some family members deserted others during the Black Death.

Disease can have long-term results. An example is the Peasants' Revolt in England. It happened thirty years after the Black Death had made peasants more aware of improving their working conditions.

Disease can have short-term results. An example is the spending spree poor people went on after the Black Death in Europe.

Disease puts scientists into labs to do research. A lot of money is spent on this. Scientists try to find out whether their theories are true or not. An example is the research being done on flu. Does it come from outer space as one theory suggests? Why do so many strains seem to come from China where people live in close contact with ducks and pigs which carry the viruses? Scientists borrow information from past epidemics such as the Black Death to help them find a plan to cope with the next epidemic.

Epidemics can cause different reactions. An example is the way some people ran away from the Black Death while others tried to hep the sick.

Epidemics can show how authorities have not looked after people properly. An example is the 1994 plague in India. It showed that cities were full of garbage and pollution.

Diseases can cause arguments among groups in societies. An example is the argument over vaccinations in New Zealand.

Epidemics can make people scared. They look about for others to blame. An example is the way Jews were persecuted by Christians during the Black Death.

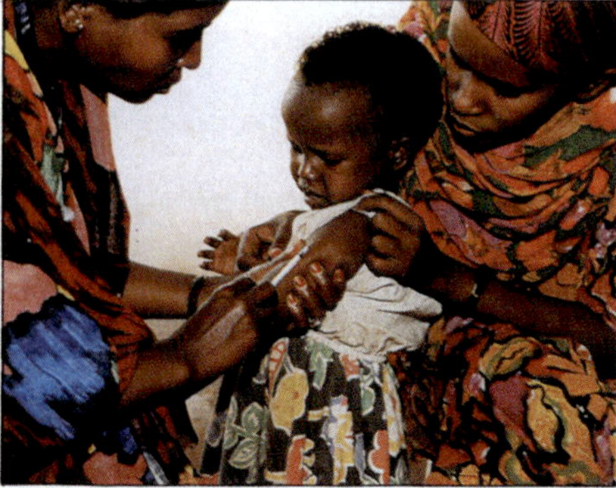

SKILL / PŪKENGA

Creating a Chart

With your group, make a chart of some of the main results of epidemics. Use the word IMPACT in your title. Make your chart as eye-catching as possible. Think of ways to show how epidemics strike (like lightning? tidal waves? arrows?).

Exploring Values Through a Debate

Topic for debate –

That epidemics are nature's way of keeping the population of the world at a manageable level.